c.1

DATE DUE $15.95

796.342
Ede   Edelson, Paula
       Superstars of men's tennis

MALE SPORTS STARS

CHELSEA HOUSE PUBLISHERS

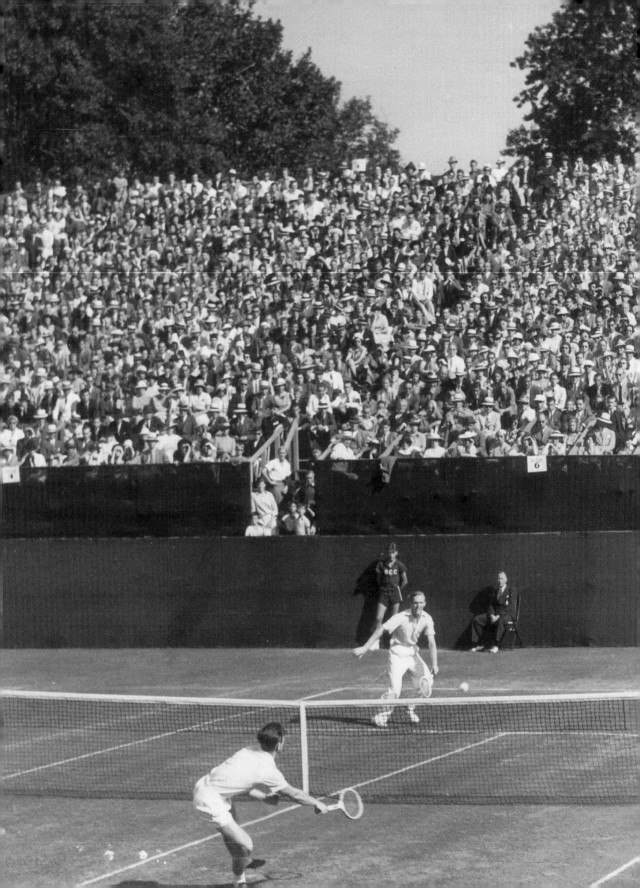

MALE SPORTS STARS

SUPERSTARS OF MEN'S TENNIS

Paula Edelson

CHELSEA HOUSE PUBLISHERS
Philadelphia

Produced by Daniel Bial and Associates
New York, New York

Picture research by Alan Gottlieb
Cover illustration by Bill Vann

First Printing

1 3 5 7 9 8 6 4 2

Library of Congress Cataloging-in-Publication Data

Edelson, Paula.
    Superstars of men's tennis / Paula Edelson.
        p. cm. — (Male sports stars)
    Includes bibliographical references (p.) and index.
    Summary: Provides a brief look at some of the major players in
men's tennis, from the late 1800s to the 1990s.
    ISBN 0-7910-4590-0 (hardcover)
    1. Tennis players—Biography—Juvenile literature. [1. Tennis
players.] I. Title. II. Series.
GV994.A1E34   1998
796.342'081'0922—dc21
[B]   97–41068
                                                   CIP
                                                   AC

CONTENTS

THE EARLY YEARS

Chances are, you've seen at least one tennis match on television. Maybe it was a contest between two of today's best male players. Have you ever watched Andre Agassi play Pete Sampras? Or Sampras play Boris Becker? If you have, you know how fast and exciting men's tennis can be.

What you may not know is that tennis has been around for a long time. It was first played in England about 500 years ago. In those days, it was a game played outside on a lawn, usually by members of the royal family. Since that time, tennis has become one of the most popular sports and is played in all parts of the world.

These days, tennis players play in many tournaments each year, but there are four major ones, known as "Grand Slam" events. These tournaments are the All-England Championships, played in Wimbledon, Great Britain; the United

Bill Tilden was tennis's first superstar. To this day, some people say he was the greatest player ever.

States Championships, played in Flushing Meadow, New York; the French Championships, played in Paris, France, and the Australian Championships, played in Melbourne, Australia. Then there is the prestigious Davis Cup tournament, which is a competition played each year by a team of players representing a nation. The United States won the first Davis Cup competition, which was played in 1900.

The oldest of the Grand Slam tournaments, the All-England Championships (known as Wimbledon), began in 1877. The only event held that year was the Gentleman's Singles competition. Spencer Gore, an Englishman, defeated 21 other competitors to win the first Wimbledon title.

In 1997, by contrast, more than 200 players entered the Gentleman's Singles championships at Wimbledon. All four "Grand Slam" events feature five competitions. There are singles and doubles championships for both men and women, and there is a mixed doubles event that pairs a man and a woman on each side.

There have been other changes in tennis since the late 19th century. For one thing, winning a Grand Slam event today immediately makes a player rich and famous. In 1985, for example, no one had ever heard of a seventeen-year-old German player named Boris Becker. But Becker surprised the world by becoming the youngest man ever to win the Gentleman's Singles title at Wimbledon. Almost overnight, he became a household name. His face was seen on magazine covers and in commercials in both Europe and the United States. By the following year, Becker was one of the highest-paid and most well known male players in the world.

But had Becker been playing tennis in the first

part of the twentieth century, chances are he would not have climbed to fame so quickly. Until the 1950s, there were no radio or television broadcasts of tennis matches. People who wanted to watch tennis had to go to the site of a tournament and see it live. For that reason, there was a much smaller following for tennis than there was for, say, baseball, which did have radio coverage.

In addition, until 1968, there was a rule that tennis players who wanted to compete in one of the Grand Slam events could not be paid for playing tennis. Believe it or not, players during those days were not allowed to receive money for winning the most competitive tennis tournaments in the world. The issue of whether these athletes could or should be allowed to be "professional" is a very important part of the history of tennis. It's an issue you'll learn more about as you read this book. But in the meantime, it's important to know that many of the men described in this book began their careers as amateurs, playing tennis not only because they were excellent competitors, but out of a sheer love of the sport itself. The first of these players, William Tatem (Bill) Tilden, was not only a master of the game but a tennis pioneer who brought tennis to a new level, both on and off the court.

BILL TILDEN: THE FIRST GREAT AMERICAN PLAYER

In 1920, most people thought of tennis as a leisure activity for the upper classes—a game only rich people played. To a certain extent, this was true. Those who played tennis usually did so at country clubs or expensive resorts.

Bill Tilden was no exception to this rule. Born in 1893 to a wealthy Philadelphia family, Tilden learned the game of tennis at his family's country club and at a resort in the Catskill mountains of New York, where the Tildens spent their summers.

But there was one major way in which Tilden was an exception. Unlike most of the people he played against during his early years, Bill Tilden took the sport of tennis seriously. In those days, people didn't put tennis in the same category as sports such as baseball, football, and basketball. Instead, tennis was viewed as something people did to relax and enjoy being outdoors.

Bill Tilden had other ideas. Tall and athletic, he worked constantly to increase the power of his serve and his speed around the court. His friends noticed his dedication. One day Frank Deacon, who played with Tilden on the high school tennis team, saw Tilden practicing and told him to take it easy. "Deacon," Tilden answered without looking up, "I'll play my own sweet game."

And play it he did. Tilden won his first Wimbledon title in 1920 and also captured the U.S. championship that year. Between 1920 and 1930 he would win two more Wimbledon and five more U.S. titles, and he ranked as the country's number-one player throughout the entire decade.

During those years Tilden constantly worked on his game. He developed shots, such as backhand and forehand topspin strokes, that had never been seen before, and he was the first player to use the entire court with expertise. He had few weaknesses and great determination. He also won far more matches than he lost. In the 1920s

Tilden played 22 Davis Cup contests and emerged victorious in 17 of them.

In 1930 Tilden turned professional, which meant he could be paid to play tennis. But since he was no longer an amateur, he could not play on the American Davis Cup team or compete in any of the Grand Slam events. But Tilden was successful anyway, winning 340 matches and losing only 147 between 1931 and 1935.

Tilden's success brought a lot of attention to the game of tennis. People enjoyed seeing him play, because of his sportsmanship (he would sometimes argue calls on his opponents' behalf) and his tremendous athletic ability. Tilden's matches were entertaining as well as competitive. On several occasions he came from far behind to win, which kept the fans interested and excited. During the 1920s, Tilden was as important to tennis as Babe Ruth was to baseball and was almost as famous as well. He died in 1953, at the age of 60.

ALL FOR ONE: THE FRENCH "FOUR MUSKETEERS"

Bill Tilden won many championships during the 1920s, but he didn't win all of them. He had very strong competition, not from just one player, but from four. Rene Lacoste, Jacques Brugnon, Jean Borotra, and Henri Cochet were known as the "four musketeers." As a team, they won six straight Davis Cup championships for France in the late 1920s and early 1930s.

Individually they did very well, too. Born in Lyon, France, in 1902, Henri Cochet won his first Grand Slam tournament at the age of 20, when he won the French Championships in 1922. Between 1922 and 1932, Cochet would win five French titles. But what some Americans remember most about Henri Cochet didn't happen in Paris, but in Forest Hills, New York, at the United States Championships in 1926. Cochet surprised the crowd on hand—and the entire nation—by beating Bill Tilden, who had won six straight titles, in the quarterfinals. Cochet did not win the U.S. title that year, but he did win the tournament in 1928. He also won Wimbledon twice—in 1927 and 1929. Cochet's total of eight Grand Slam tournament titles makes him the winningest of the musketeers.

Lacoste, probably the most famous of the four, was born in Paris in 1904. As a child, Lacoste was extremely frail and suffered from asthma. He certainly didn't look like an athlete, much less a future tennis champion. When he was 15, his father suggested that he give up sports completely. But Lacoste continued to play, and he got better and stronger as he grew up. He won his first United States Championship in 1926, when he beat Cochet. The next year he defended his title by defeating Tilden in one of the most famous matches ever played. The two battled back and forth for more than an hour and a half. Tilden held set point a total of six times, but Lacoste ended up winning by a score of 11-9, 6-3, 11-9 (there were no tiebreakers in those days). Known worldwide as "The Crocodile," Lacoste was one of the first players to use a ball machine during practice—something he did almost every day, even after playing a tournament match. He went on to win seven Grand Slam tournaments. He also became a wealthy businessman, selling

Jean Borotra (left) and Rene Lacoste, two of the "four muske-teers," teamed up to play dou-bles at the 1925 U.S. doubles championships.

shirts with his characteristic crocodile on it—which are still popular today.

Borotra was born in 1905 in Basque, which is in southwestern France, near the border of Spain. Of all the musketeers, Borotra might have been the most fun to watch on the court. He could move very quickly, especially when he was close to the net. Many people believe Borotra had one of the best volley shots (a shot that's hit before the ball bounces) in tennis. Borotra's ability to leap for balls that seemed out his reach earned him the nickname "The Bouncing Basque." He won the French Championship in 1924 and again in 1931, for a total of two individual Grand Slam tournament titles.

Like Lacoste, Jacques Brugnon was raised in Paris. He was born there in 1895, making him the oldest musketeer. Called "Toto" by his friends, Brugnon was known as the leader of the musketeers. He could always be depended on to help his teammates when they needed a practice partner. Brugnon did not win any Grand Slam events as a singles player—he didn't enjoy singles as much as his teammates did. What Brugnon really liked was the doubles game. Paired with one or another of his musketeer teammates, Brugnon won 10 Grand Slam tournament doubles crowns.

FRED PERRY: THE PRIDE OF BRITAIN

The four musketeers ruled the tennis courts until the early 1930s, when Lacoste retired. Suddenly there was room for a new champion, and an Englishman named Fred Perry quickly rose to the occasion.

Born in London in 1910, Perry became a champion with racket and ball while still a teenager. However, young Fred's earliest title was not won in tennis but in table tennis, or ping pong. Representing Great Britain at the Budapest Championships in 1929, Perry came away with the table tennis world title.

Perry's ping pong skills came in handy when he started playing tennis at the age of 14. He had excellent instincts and moved to the ball quickly—talents that he most certainly developed as a tennis table player. He also had powerful groundstrokes, including a running forehand that became one of his most famous shots. Perry played his first Davis Cup match in 1931, at the age of 21. Two years later, he led Great

Britain to the first of four consecutive Davis Cup titles.

From 1933 to 1936, Perry completely dominated men's amateur tennis. He won the Australian title in 1934 and the French Championship in 1935, and he took U.S. honors in 1933, 1934, and 1936. But Perry is most remembered for his three consecutive Wimbledon titles, won in 1934, 1935, and 1936. It's a feat that was not repeated until Bjorn Borg won five consecutive Wimbledon titles between 1976 and 1980. More important, perhaps, Perry's victories marked the last time an Englishman won the British title. In the more than 60 years since, the Wimbledon Gentleman's Singles title has gone to a champion from another country.

Perry was still at the top of his game when he turned professional in 1937. This meant, of course, that he could no longer compete in either the Davis Cup or any of the Grand Slam events. If he had remained on the amateur circuit, though, he would have battled the man who would dominate tennis over the next couple of years—a Californian named Don Budge.

Fred Perry jumps high for a slam during the 1936 U.S. Championship. He beat Ernest Sutter here and eventually won the tournament.

In 1938, Don Budge became the first player to win tennis's Grand Slam—the Australian, French, and U.S. championships, plus Wimbledon.

DON BUDGE: MISTER GRAND SLAM

John Donald Budge was born in Oakland, California, in 1916. His family had recently emigrated to America from Scotland, where Don's father played professional soccer.

As a boy, Don played many sports. Tennis, he said later, was the one he liked the least. In fact, when he was 11, Don decided he would never play tennis again. He put down his racket, he thought, for good. But four years later he picked it up again. Encouraged by his brother and first tennis partner, Lloyd, Don entered his first tournament in 1931—and won it. He was 15 years old.

In 1935, Budge played on the United States Davis Cup team. He won all his matches, but the U.S. team eventually lost to Germany, that year's champion.

During this time Budge worked hard on his game. One of his greatest influences was Fred Perry. Budge admired Perry's groundstrokes and quickness on the court. Perry graciously coached Budge on several occasions, teaching him a more effective backhand and also an approach shot, which is the shot a player makes while running toward the net.

By 1937, Budge was not only a complete tennis player, but the finest one on the amateur circuit. That year he won both the Wimbledon and U.S. championships. He also led the U.S. to the Davis Cup by defeating a German, Gottfried Von Cramm, in what many believe was the greatest tennis match ever played. Down two sets to none, Budge rallied back to defeat Von Cramm by a final score of 6-8, 5-7, 6-4, 6-2, 8-6.

But Budge saved his greatest achievement for the following year. Only two men in the history of tennis have ever won all four Grand Slam events in one year. In 1938, at the age of 22, Don Budge became the first to sweep the Grand Slam events when he won the Wimbledon, U.S., French, and Australian titles. (Rod Laver is the only other player to accomplished this feat. He did it in 1962 and again in 1969.)

The following year, Budge did what Perry and Tilden had done before him: he turned professional. Over a nine-year span, amateur tennis lost three top competitors, who ended up playing each other quite often as professionals.

2
THE PRE-OPEN ERA

Born in Las Vegas in 1921, Jack Kramer burst onto the international tennis scene in 1939, when he became the youngest competitor to play in a challenge round at the Davis Cup. He and Joe Hunt lost in doubles to the Australian tandem of John Bromwich and Adrian Quist. On the very day of that match, Great Britain declared war on Germany, marking the beginning of World War II. That four-year conflict would claim the lives of several top-ranked tennis players, including Kramer's doubles partner, Hunt.

But Kramer was luckier than many of his fellow players. He enlisted in the Coast Guard and served on a war ship in the Pacific from 1942 until 1946. During those years, Kramer made up his mind to take the game of tennis more seriously. It wasn't that Kramer didn't work hard

Jack Kramer lost several of his prime tennis years while serving in the Coast Guard during World War II. After the war, his big game helped him win the U.S. Championship in 1946 and 1947 and Wimbledon in 1947.

at the sport before that time, but he did manage to get his share of drinking and gambling in as well. All that ended, though, when Kramer returned to tennis after the war.

Kramer brought more than a new attitude back with him. His "big game" approach to tennis added a new facet to the sport. Many of Kramer's contemporaries were strategists rather than power players, preferring to keep the ball in play and win when their opponents made mistakes. Kramer believed in a more aggressive approach. When asked what that approach was, Kramer answered simply: "Attack!" Rather than playing long points and switching from offensive to defensive positions on the court, Kramer hit the ball deep and hard, keeping his opponent on the defensive from the beginning of the point to the end. He also got up to the net as often as he could, where his sharp-angled volleys and vicious overheads overwhelmed his competition. In order to pull off this "big game" style of play, Kramer was constantly in motion. Even when returning serve, his feet were tapping the surface of the court, ready to move from side to side and to bring him into the net on a deep approach.

If this style of play sounds familiar to you, it's because all top-ranking tennis players (male and female) use Kramer's "big game" approach today. Whether they are serve-and-volley players such as Pete Sampras or baseline smashers like Andre Agassi, the most successful tennis players are constantly on the attack and constantly in motion. Whether they know it or not, they have Jack Kramer to thank for making tennis a faster and more aggressive sport.

In 1946 Kramer won the U.S. title—his first Grand Slam singles victory (an accomplished doubles player as well, Kramer had won two U.S. doubles crowns, in 1940 and 1941). In 1946 he also led the American team to the first of four straight Davis Cup victories. He added another U.S. title in 1947, and won Wimbledon that year as well.

But in 1948 Kramer entered what would be the competition of his life—the battle to bring credibility to professional tennis. That year, Kramer gave up his amateur status and started a professional league of his own. Not only did Kramer play in this new league, but he promoted it as well. In so doing, he managed to lure some of the game's top players, such as Frank Sedgeman, Pancho Segura, Pancho Gonzales, and Bobby Riggs. Not only did Kramer sign these players to what were then considered to be lucrative deals, but he managed to beat all of them as well, on a regular basis.

Each year Kramer would scout the Grand Slam competitions and Davis Cup matches for amateur players. By the late 1950s, rumors were floating that he was getting ready to sign the entire Australian Davis Cup team to play for his professional league. When they heard about this, Australian officials complained to the International Lawn Tennis Federation (ILTF). Composed of members from more than 90 countries, the ILTF held near-complete control over the rules and regulations of competitive tennis. The ILTF decided to act, and it prohibited Kramer's league from playing in that country's leading clubs.

Kramer stopped playing tennis in 1960, but his league continued to survive in the 1960s and to battle amateur tennis for attention and prestige. In 1968, Kramer's cause achieved a major victory when professionals were at last allowed to play in the major competitions (with the exception of the Davis Cup). Kramer himself went on to serve on the board of the ILTF, the very association he had battled for so many years, and he later became the executive director of the Association of Tennis Professionals (ATP). Brash, aggressive, and supremely confident from the beginning of his career to the end, Kramer used his "big game" approach to change the sport of tennis, both on and off the court.

BOBBY RIGGS: KING OF STRATEGY

When people think of Bobby Riggs today, several words come to mind right away. Gambler. Chauvinist. Showman. These descriptions may be accurate, but it's also true that in his day Riggs was a successful tennis player on both the amateur and professional circuits.

Born in Los Angeles in 1918, Riggs was the fifth and youngest son of a minister. He began playing tennis in high school and achieved great success with a game plan completely different from the "big game" approach of Jack Kramer. Rather than attack the ball from beginning to end of a point, Riggs played the on-court strategist. He rarely made mistakes, and he played wisely and patiently until his opponent would finally make an error. Riggs's patience was so long-lasting that, according to legend, it once took him more than two hours to beat an opponent 6-0, 6-0, 6-0.

A little known fact about Riggs is that he was the player who succeeded Don Budge as the world's number-one player. He achieved this status in 1939, when he won both the Wimbledon

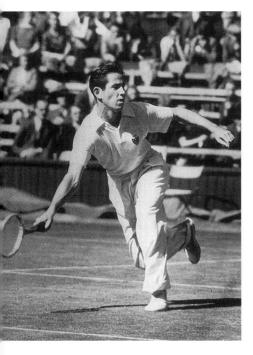

Bobby Riggs was shorter than most great tennis players. But he was able to use his quickness and cunning to defeat players who could serve and hit harder.

and U.S. titles. He went on to win one more Grand Slam event, when he took U.S. honors again in 1941.

Even during those years, Riggs was as well known for gambling as for being a good tennis player. His behavior off the court kept him in constant trouble with the ILTF. Its members were no doubt relieved when Riggs relinquished his amateur status in 1946—one year before Kramer spearheaded his professional league. Riggs held his own on the professional circuit. Although he was usually no match for Kramer himself, Riggs outplayed Don Budge on a regular basis and won three professional titles in his career.

But there's no denying that Riggs is best remembered for the match he played one autumn evening in 1973. His opponent that night was not a man, but a woman named Billie Jean King. Riggs had already destroyed Margaret Court Smith, the first winner of the women's Grand Slam, in the first major intersex battle. But when Riggs tried to repeat the challenge against the brash, aggressive play of Billie Jean King, King showed that she could outhustle, outsmash, and outsmart the one-time number-one male player.

PANCHO GONZALES: SERVE-AND-VOLLEY ACE

Bobby Riggs may have provided strategy on the court, but the greatest talent to challenge Jack Kramer during the 1940s was a Mexican American named Pancho Gonzales.

Born in Los Angeles in 1928, Richard "Pancho" Gonzales grew up in a very poor section of the city. It's surprising that someone from such an impoverished area would go on to achieve success in what had always been known as a rich person's sport, but from the time he was a teenager it was clear that Gonzales's tennis talent was worth its weight in gold. By the time he was 15, Gonzales was the top-ranked tennis player his age in Southern California. Even though he was a good student, he decided to quit school to concentrate on the sport. But when his principal found out what young Richard's plan was, he barred Gonzales from all state-wide tournaments, declaring that it was unfair for a person who practiced tennis all day long to compete against players who were in school all day.

This incident stayed with Gonzales for many years. Rather than returning to school, he opted to join the Navy, where he served for 15 months. When he returned to civilian life, Gonzales began playing tennis competitively again. Tall and thin, Gonzales combined speed, agility, and power to overwhelm his opponents. According to legend, no one traveled to the net more quickly than Gonzales could, and his overhead smashes were so overwhelming that they were rarely returned. Even more impressive were his serves. Throughout his career Gonzales was known to have the most fluid and powerful service delivery on any tennis court. For this reason, he was able to take the serve-and-volley game to new heights.

Gonzales's remarkable talents earned him the U.S. Championship in 1947 and 1948. He failed to win any Grand Slam events in 1949, but he did play for the triumphant American team in that year's Davis Cup tournament. The next year, he quit the amateur ranks to play for Jack Kramer's professional league. Gonzales won several professional titles over the next 18 years,

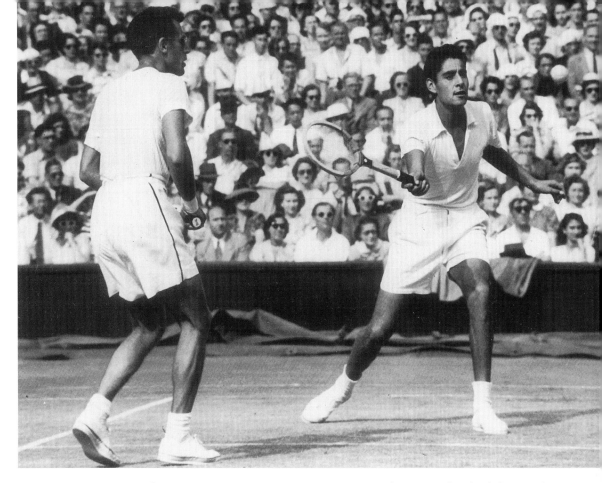

but he quit the professional circuit to return to the amateur ranks in 1967. The following year, when the Open Era officially began, Gonzales was still active and a formidable force on the court.

Although Gonzales won his share of titles during his long career, there's little doubt that had he remained an amateur, he would have won many more Grand Slam events during the early 1950s. Gonzales's talents were recognized by many sports enthusiasts, and any list of the greatest tennis players of all time always includes him. Unfortunately for tennis, many of the sport's greatest talents did not play in the major tournaments during the prime of their careers, choosing to play professionally instead.

Pancho Gonzales (right) was the first Hispanic American to become a tennis superstar. Here the team of Gonzales and Frank Parker (players who each won two U.S. Championships) win the 1949 Wimbledon doubles championship.

3

THE OPEN ERA BEGINS

In 1968, Robert Kennedy and Martin Luther King were both murdered by assassins' bullets. The Vietnam War was tearing the nation apart, as millions marched in protest of America's involvement in that campaign. Richard Nixon was elected president, and America's space program was in the process of preparing a rocket that, one year later, would put a man on the moon for the first time in history.

Against this background, the change that occurred in tennis might not seem significant. But in fact, 1968 was the most important year in the modern history of tennis for one simple reason. That was the first year that professional players were legally allowed to enter the game's most prestigious tournaments.

Men's tennis in the late 1950s and 1960s was dominated by the "Aussie Invasion." Australian stars included (from left to right) Rod Laver, Ken Rosewall, and Tony Roche. To the right is Tom Okker of Holland.

In other words, 1968 marked the beginning of the "open era" in tennis. When used in this sense, the word "open" means that these competitions were "open," or available, to all qualified tennis players, regardless of whether they were professionals or amateurs. The events leading up to this decision were complicated. At one point in 1960, the change was on the verge of becoming official. The ILTF had gathered in Paris to vote on lifting its regulations against professionals, and many players such as Pancho Gonzales fully expected the vote to pass. Gonzales was surprised and angry when he learned that the measure had lost by three votes. It was discovered later that one member of the ILTF known to be in favor of lifting the regulation was in the bathroom at the time the vote was held; another had fallen asleep; and a third was not in attendance at all, for reasons unknown.

Seven years later, however, the circumstances and the outcome were quite different. By this time, the cause to "open" tennis to professionals had a new champion in Herman David, the president of the All-England Tennis Association, the club that held Wimbledon every year. Earlier that year, David had already made a bold move by running a professional tournament on the Centre Court at Wimbledon. Although it was not quite the same thing as opening the Wimbledon championship itself to the professional players, it still spoke volumes about where tennis was headed. Sure enough, in December of 1967 the British Lawn Tennis Association (BLTA), headed by David, voted by a lopsided margin of 295-5 to open the 1968 Wimbledon tournament to professionals as well as amateurs.

Although the BLTA had passed this measure, there was no guarantee that the ILTF would agree to it. But under pressure of losing their most prestigious tournament, the bigger association did back down, and during a special meeting in Paris in March of 1968, the ILTF finally passed the measure that brought about the open era in tennis. Professionals were now allowed to play in the sport's Grand Slam events. Tennis would never be the same.

One unexpected change was the sudden emergence of Australian players on the international scene. In addition to those profiled below, star players included Fred Stolle, Neale Fraser, and Roy Emerson, who holds the record for most major victories—12. Emerson won the Australian Open six times, and he won twice at each of the three other major sites.

KEN ROSEWALL: IN HIS PRIME AT THE WRONG TIME

Born in Sydney, Australia in 1934, Ken Rosewall was the only child of two tennis-playing parents. His father so loved the sport, in fact, that when Ken was still a baby he bought a piece of land with three tennis courts on it. He supplemented his income by renting out the courts to local players.

Rosewall entered his first Davis Cup competition in 1952, and the following year he led the Australian squad to victory. That was also the year that Rosewall played in his first Grand Slam event, when he upset Vic Seixas, the number-one-seeded player, in the fourth round at the

Rod Laver seems to do a pirouette in returning a ball against fellow Australian Bob Hewitt at the 1961 Wimbledon. Laver would win the first of his four Wimbledon titles that year.

U.S. championships. (Rosewall would eventually lose in the semifinals.) Rosewall would go on to win the 1953 French Championship, the Australian title in 1953 and 1955, and U.S. honors in 1956. Unlike many of his contemporaries who relied on the serve-and-volley game, Rosewall found his greatest success by staying on the baseline and bashing accurately placed shots all over the court. This is not to say that he could not move to the net and win a point with a volley when he wanted to, but Rosewall preferred to use his quickness and accuracy in the backcourt.

In 1956, Rosewall did what virtually every other amateur champion did during the pre-open era—he gave up his eligibility to win more Grand Slam events by turning professional. He found great success on the professional tour, playing against the likes of Jack Kramer, Pancho Gonzales, and his fellow countryman Rod Laver.

But in 1968, when the open era finally began, Rosewall was already 34 and beyond his prime. He did, however, manage to win the French Open in 1968 and to take top honors in Australia in 1971 and 1972. Rosewall made his final appearance in a Grand Slam event when he reached the Wimbledon final in 1974. He lost in straight sets to a young left-handed American named Jimmy Connors.

ROD LAVER: ROCKET

Rosewall was only one of several Australians to rock the tennis world during the years directly leading up to and following the beginning of the open era. In fact, one of those down-under players, a savvy left-hander named Rod Laver, proved to be among the most dominating competitors ever to grace a tennis court.

Rod Laver was born on a farm in Gladstone, Australia, in 1938. He was a small and sickly child and never did grow up to become an overpowering player. At the height of his game he stood 5'8" and weighed about 150 pounds. But despite his size, Laver dominated tennis so forcefully during the 1960s that the press dubbed him "Rod the Rocket," and he was called simply "Rocket" by all of his Australian teammates. Rather than overpowering the ball, Laver used his magnificent wrist flexibility and quick short strokes to flick winners across the net from any part of the court.

Laver burst onto the tennis scene in 1959, when at the age of 21 he became the Australian singles and doubles champion and went on to play for his country in the Davis Cup. It was the first of eight Davis Cup appearances for Laver, and with Rocket on the team Australia would win seven championships.

One year later, in 1960, Laver won his first Grand Slam event when he won the Australian title. The following year he won the French championship, and in 1962 Laver did what no player had achieved since Don Budge in 1938: he won tennis's Grand Slam by taking all four major

Big John Newcombe was the youngest and strongest of the "Aussie Invasion." Here he holds the trophy after winning Wimbledon in 1971.

tournaments. Following this historic achievement, Laver joined his countryman Ken Rosewall on the professional circuit, where he played with great success for the next four years.

But in 1967, Laver returned to amateur play. He missed the grandeur and sheer competition of the Grand Slam events and was not making enough money on the professional circuit, which by then was not as lucrative as it had once been. The following year, Laver's move paid off for him as the open era officially began. Laver celebrated his now legitimate professional status by winning the first Wimbledon open championship in 1968.

The following year was an even more impressive one for Rocket. Now 31 years of age, he was one of the elder statesman on the tennis circuit. But there was still plenty of fight and flight left in the Australian master of the game. With his superb wrist flicks, fleet footwork, and sterling volleys, Laver dominated the sport once more, winning all four of 1969's Grand Slam events. With that achievement, Laver became not only the first player to win the Grand Slam twice, but the first and only player to do so as both an amateur (in 1962) and as a professional (in 1969).

Laver retired from tennis shortly after his historic feat. Almost twenty years later, he remains one of the legends of the game. Few players, past or present, have matched his instincts and quickness on the court.

JOHN NEWCOMBE: STRAPPING POWER

A third Australian came to tennis's forefront at this time: John Newcombe, the most powerful of the "Aussie invasion." Born in 1944, Newcombe won the Southeastern Australian title at the age of 19 in 1963. That same year, he was named to the Australian Davis Cup team, the first of six consecutive appearances he made. Five out of those six years, Australia took home the Davis cup—a tribute not only to Newcombe's strapping power on the court, but also to his leadership and presence off of it. No doubt about it—John Newcombe was a winner.

Newcombe's greatest attribute on the court was a huge, heavy, and loping serve that often overpowered his opponents. However, Newcombe was equipped not only with great strength but with a strategic and intelligent mind. Just when a player was most prepared to receive and return a blistering Newcombe shot, Big John would suddenly take the pace off the ball, leaving his opponent bewildered, flatfooted, and endlessly frustrated.

Newcombe's strategy, power, and mind control—he was said to possess remarkable concentration and was seldom upset on or off the court—helped him become a dominating force on the amateur circuit during the 1960s and early 1970s. He won the title at Wimbledon in 1967, 1970, and 1971; was the U.S. champion in 1967 and 1973; and took Australian honors in 1975.

One of the reasons Newcombe won so many Grand Slam events was that he remained an amateur up until 1968, when the open era began.

At the time Newcombe was in his prime, the professional circuit was not paying its players the way it once had been, and the most gifted competitors, such as Laver and Gonzales, were actually returning to the amateur circuit. Newcombe managed to win events both as an amateur and a professional, and his gracious style of play combined with good strategy and awesome power made him a valuable part of the very dominating Australian teams of the late 1960s.

ARTHUR ASHE: MAN FOR ALL SEASONS

It was one of the greatest events of the year. For the first time in its history, the tournament at Forest Hills was open to professionals. The great players of the decade turned out in full force and played their hearts out, all of them fully expecting to win. And when the dust had cleared, the first men's U.S. Open crown was won by an amateur—a young American by the name of Arthur Ashe.

When Ashe scored the final point of his five-match victory (14-12, 5-7, 6-3, 3-6, 6-3) over Tom Okker in 1968, he became the first black man ever to win a Grand Slam event. (Althea Gibson became the first black Grand Slam tournament champion when she won the French crown in 1956.) It was a defining moment for all of tennis, but for Ashe, it was just one of many victories.

Arthur Ashe Jr. was born in Richmond, Virginia, in 1943. At the time Arthur was born, his father was a chauffeur, though he later worked his way up in the world, becoming first a police officer and eventually head of his own land-

Arthur Ashe's greatest victory came when he defeated Tom Okker to win the 1968 U.S. Open.

scaping and custodial business. Arthur Jr. began playing tennis at the age of seven, and when he was 10, he was discovered by Dr. Robert W. Johnson, a local black doctor and tennis fan who believed in supporting and sponsoring young black tennis talent. Under the guiding hand of Dr. Johnson, Ashe learned not only how to hit powerful groundstrokes and sharp-angled volleys, but how to conduct himself on and off the court with grace and good manners.

Arthur needed all the support he could get; growing up in the South during the 1940s and 1950s was a difficult experience for any black person. Segregation was the rule, and blacks were excluded from white restaurants, schools, and country clubs.

Ashe won his first tennis title at the age of 17, when he took top honors at the United States Indoor Junior Championships in 1960. He was the first black male player to do so. Three years later, he made history again, becoming the first black person to play on the American Davis Cup team. That year he won his first of what would be 27 Davis Cup singles matches—a record that would hold until John McEnroe came along and won 41. Ashe's remarkable Davis Cup career also included a five-year stint as captain of the men's squad, from 1981 through 1985.

It was, in fact, Ashe's desire to keep playing Davis Cup tennis that kept him from turning professional in 1968. While all other tournaments had opened up to professional players, the Davis Cup remained an amateur-only event. And so it was that when Ashe beat Okker in that marathon U.S. Open final, he brought home only a fraction of the money that Okker did.

But for Arthur Ashe, money was never a key reason to play tennis. Much more important to him was the sport itself, which he mastered as well as anyone of his generation. His backhand was considered to be the most dangerous of anyone playing during his time, and he was one of the most effective serve-and-volleyers on the tennis circuit. As significant, Ashe played his game strategically and intelligently. He was one of the first players to review tapes of his competitors in order to figure out the best way to play and defeat them. Ashe's approach to the game netted him not only the 1968 U.S. Open title but top honors at Wimbledon in 1975, when he defeated Jimmy Connors in a well-remembered four-set match.

Ashe spent a great deal of his time acting as an ambassador for the sport of tennis. This mission took him to several continents over the course of a few years, as he traveled to all parts of the world (including South Africa, then under the segregating force of apartheid) playing exhibitions and representing his country both on and off the court.

Arthur Ashe faced his toughest and final battle against AIDS, which he contracted through contaminated blood transfusions during open heart surgery in 1983. Typical of Ashe, he fought the disease with grace and dignity. He died of complications from AIDS in 1992.

4

THE POPULARITY OF TENNIS EXPLODES

When Billie Jean King embarrassed Bobby Riggs in the Battle of the Sexes on September 30, 1973, she not only struck a blow for women's equality, but her straight set victory (6-4, 6-3, 6-3) did more to promote American tennis than any single match in history.

During the next few years, tennis would take off as both a participatory and spectator sport. King would help sponsor and promote a new national tennis league known as World Team Tennis, with teams from 10 cities competing against each other during the spring and summer. World Team Tennis eventually failed, but it did have some successful years during the mid-1970s.

In the meantime, control in the men's game was slowly moving from Australia, where Laver, Newcombe, and Rosewall had dominated the

Jimmy Connors always played with a lot of heart—and loved to stoke up the crowd to root for him.

sport during the 1960s, back to the Western Hemisphere. Two Americans and one Swede would spend the 1970s battling for top positioning in what was becoming an ever more powerful, exciting, and popular sport.

JIMMY CONNORS: GOTTA WIN

He was a player fans loved to hate. His aggression was never hidden on the court, partly because he made no effort to conceal his desire to win each and every match he played. For James Scott Connors, every match was do or die, and it was that iron will that made him controversial with the crowds and immensely successful on the court.

Connors was born in East St. Louis, Illinois, in 1952. His parents divorced when he was very young, and Jimmy and his brother John were brought up by their mother, Gloria, a tennis enthusiast and teacher. It was Gloria and her mother, Bertha (whom Connors lovingly referred to as "Two Mom"), who taught Jimmy and John the fundamentals of the game. When he was 12, John Connors decided that tennis was not for him and quit playing for good. Jimmy, on the other hand, inherited his mother's and grandmother's love for the sport and began playing junior tournaments—and winning most of them.

In 1971, Connors played his first Grand Slam tournaments, reaching the quarterfinals of both Wimbledon and the U.S. Open. No one on the men's tour at the time played tennis quite like Connors did. Most of the players had adapted Jack Kramer's "big game" style of competing. This type of tennis, played by Laver, Newcombe, and Ashe among others, relied upon a strong serve-and-volley game. Connors, by contrast, thrived on the baseline. His bread and butter stroke was his powerful two-handed backhand. Connors was, in fact, the first male player to use that stroke successfully. It was considered at the time to be a woman's stroke, and in fact Connors' entire game was more familiar to the women's tour than to the men's. This is no coincidence, considering that Connors' original teachers were women. But make no mistake—Connors threw enough strength and power into his groundstrokes to neutralize many facets of the serve-and-volley game. He had what was without a doubt the best service return in the game and was able to shoot two-handed winners from almost any part of the court. His game has influenced such contemporary players as Andre Agassi.

Connors was also the first top player to use a racket made of steel. Until this time, almost every racket was made of wood, a material that didn't add power to shots but did give players the ability to control their shots and place them with great accuracy. Steel rackets were a much more powerful weapon, but most players couldn't find a way to use the additional speed without sacrificing control. Connors usually made more unforced errors than his opponents, but the power of his strokes won him more points than he lost.

Eventually, of course, players did make the change from wood rackets—first to metal (Arthur Ashe began using one in the mid-1970s) and finally to graphite. Connors was the first to make the proper adjustments to his game. As a result, he hit the ball harder than anyone else in the

1970s.

But at least as powerful as Connors' strokes was his will to win. Although at 5'10" and 150 pounds he was one of the smallest competitors on the tour, he was never intimidated by bigger or stronger players. That kind of attitude has made him one of the most successful Americans ever to play the game. Connors won his first Grand Slam event early in 1974, when he took top honors at the Australian Open. Five months later he completely dominated Ken Rosewall at Wimbledon, then won the U.S. Open in early September. Three Grand Slam tournaments in one year—tennis hadn't seen a performance like it since Laver won all four events in 1969.

Connors would go on to win a total of eight Grand Slam tournaments. Five of his championships would come at the U.S. Open, his favorite tournament. He would never win the French Open (he didn't play in it for five years during the mid-1970s), and he played on only two Davis Cup teams. (One of the more popular criticisms of Connors was that he was a selfish player because he usually refused to participate in Davis Cup play.) Perhaps his greatest achievement was the sheer number of matches he won at the U.S. Open. His 98 victories at this event is a record that may never be broken. He retired from competitive tennis in 1992.

BJORN BORG—
SWEDEN'S GOLDEN BOY

As Connors was dominating tennis in America, another back-court specialist was rising in the ranks on the other side of the Atlantic. His name was Bjorn Borg, and he would go on to challenge Connors for the number-one spot in what would become one of the greatest rivalries in the sport.

Born in Sodertalje, Sweden, in 1957, young Bjorn first began playing tennis at the age of seven. That year his father, Rune, a clothing salesman, won a tennis racket at a table tennis tournament and gave it to his son. The Borg family enjoyed playing sports together on weekends, and Bjorn spent many Saturdays playing against his father. During those years Borg had a very bad temper and was often sent to bed early because of the tantrums he threw. This type of discipline helped shape Borg's famously calm countenance during his professional playing years, when Borg was virtually never seen to lose his temper on the court.

Borg's natural athleticism and talent caught the eye of Percy Rosburg, then a coach for the Swedish Tennis Federation. Rosburg helped Borg strengthen his groundstrokes, adding topspin and precision to his game. At the age of 15, Borg left school in order to play tennis on a full-time basis. He entered his first Grand Slam event in 1973, when he reached the fourth round of the French Open at the age of 16. One year later, he won the French title and began compiling what is statistically the most successful Grand Slam record in tennis history.

Of the 27 Grand Slam events Borg entered between 1973 and 1981, he won 11 of them and reached the finals 16 times. Connors, by contrast, reached 14 Grand Slam finals but won

Bjorn Borg shows off his two-handed backhand. Borg won five Wimbledons in a row and retired at the age of 26.

only 8 of them. Interestingly, Borg managed those 11 titles without winning one final at either the Australian Open or the U.S. Open. He reached the final at the American tournament four times without winning. The Australian Championship he played in only once, reaching the third round in 1975. Borg was a successful Davis Cup player as well. He competed for the Swedish team from 1972 to 1975 and in 1979. In 1975, he led the Swedish team to victory, defeating the 1973 Wimbledon champion, Jan Kodes, in straight sets to clinch the title.

What is without a doubt Bjorn Borg's greatest achievement, however, was winning five consecutive Wimbledon titles from 1976 to 1980. The first of these championships came at the expense of Ilie Nastase, a Romanian player who was as well known for his antics on the court as for his talent. Nastase tried his hardest to intimidate his 19-year-old opponent, but Borg prevailed, winning the title in four sets. In 1977, Borg had to endure top competition not only from Jimmy Connors, who took him to five sets in the final, but from Vital Gerulaitis. The semifinal between Gerulaitis and Borg—friends and practice partners as well as rivals—proved to be one of the most memorable matches in Wimbledon history. Borg had a comparatively easy time winning the 1978 final—again against Connors. Borg came away with his fourth straight Wimbledon title against Roscoe Tanner, a left-handed serving specialist, then beat an up-and-coming player named John McEnroe in 1980 for Wimbledon championship number five. The following year McEnroe put an end to the record, defeating Borg in the finals.

Borg was said to hit the heaviest groundstrokes

on the tour during his prime years. His forehand topspin was so effective and bounced so high that his opponents would often have to stand several feet behind the baseline in order to return them. His two-fisted backhand was effective as well, particularly as a passing shot against overeager net players. Borg's style of playing was similar to Connors's in that they both possessed effective groundstrokes. But Borg had a twisting spin to his shots, giving him a deceptive edge that Connors's flat strokes—powerful as they were—lacked. Borg played most of his career with a wooden racket strung so tightly—a tension of 90 pounds, compared to the usual 60-to-65—that his racket frames were known to collapse from the tension of the strings.

Borg retired from tennis in 1981 a rich man. He briefly returned 10 years later in an ill-fated comeback attempt.

JOHN McENROE— BRASH AND BRILLIANT

John McEnroe was born in 1959 in Douglaston, New York. He grew up playing tennis not more than 20 miles from Flushing Meadow, now the home of the U.S. Open. He attended Stanford University on a tennis scholarship but dropped out after his sophomore year to turn professional. In 1977, McEnroe played in his first Grand Slam event, the Wimbledon championships. Most major tennis tournaments have a number of spots open to players who automatically qualify on the basis of their records. The rest of the spots must be won by unranked tennis players who play early challenge rounds. This is the way in which McEnroe entered that

Wimbledon tournament—as an unknown qualifier. He quickly made his presence known when he stunned the tennis world by reaching the semifinals.

But if McEnroe's performance that year won him raves and admiration, he was just as well remembered for his brash and rather startling on-court manner. His audible complaints over line calls and visible sulking earned him the nickname "superbrat," which stayed with him during much of his career.

McEnroe added new dimension to Jack Kramer's "big game" approach; in all of his matches, he was consistently and brilliantly on the attack. And those attacks were marked not by overpowering strength, but by quickness and deception that fooled and frustrated his opponents. His quick hands and brilliant strokes earned him seven Grand Slam tournament titles in five years, from 1979 to 1984. He captured the first of these when he took the U.S. Open title—the first of three consecutive ones—in 1979. His first Wimbledon championship came in 1981, when he ended Bjorn Borg's five-year winning streak. He repeated top honors there in 1983 and 1984. His record at the Australian Championships is unimpressive, but he did reach the finals of the French Open in 1984, when he lost a grueling five-set contest to Ivan Lendl. The final score of that match was 3-6, 2-6, 6-4, 6-4, 7-5, and it may have been McEnroe's most disappointing moment in his career. But the French Open notwithstanding, 1984 was the best year of his career. That year he won 13 singles titles (including Wimbledon and the U.S. Open) and compiled an overall record of 82-3—the best winning percentage in one year of the open era.

As important as the Grand Slam events were to McEnroe, he made time each year to participate in the Davis Cup. He played on seven consecutive American teams from 1979 to 1984, and again from 1987 to 1992. During those years the United States won three times (in 1981, 1982, and 1990). Sadly for McEnroe, his virtuoso performances in Davis Cup play were marked once again by questionable behavior in between points. He was actually cited (along with Jimmy Connors) for his poor sportsmanship in the 1984 competition. McEnroe had, according to the United States Tennis Association (USTA) report, laughed while the national anthem was being played and criticized the surface of the tennis court during the Americans' match against Sweden.

McEnroe's behavior didn't make him the most popular member of the American team, but his playing was without a doubt superior and beyond

John McEnroe flies through the air in attempt to reach a Bjorn Borg passing shot. Borg won this memorable 1980 Wimbledon final, although McEnroe broke through and won the title the next year.

Throughout his career, McEnroe seemed to get psyched up when he argued with a lineman or a crew chief.

reproach. Arthur Ashe, who captained several Davis Cup teams—and clashed with McEnroe more than once throughout those competitions—said of his playing, "McEnroe doesn't overpower or overwhelm you. He nicks you here, cuts you there, slices you somewhere else, and before you know it, you've bled to death." McEnroe had a wide range of shots, including a topspin backhand he often hit off balance and a slicing backhand that served as a deadly drop shot. His volleys were more sharply angled than overwhelming, and he was quicker to the ball—both with his hands and feet—than any player of his day.

McEnroe stopped playing tennis competitively in 1992, but he remains involved in the game, providing color commentary on television during coverage of Wimbledon and the U.S. Open—

his two favorite tournaments.

McEnroe's career spanned three decades, during which the game of tennis underwent several changes. For one thing, the location of the U.S. Open moved from the elegance and quiet of Forest Hills to the less tranquil and much louder Flushing Meadow (near New York's LaGuardia Airport).

In addition, tennis players made the change during the mid-1980s from the basic wood (or in Connors's case, steel) rackets to the larger, more flexible and more powerful weapons made of fiberglass and graphite. Some players were more hesitant to make this change than others (Connors stayed with his round-faced steel model until 1991), but all eventually began playing with the new rackets.

5

TENNIS TODAY

Tennis in the 1990s is a glamorous, big-money sport, with players who earn as much or more from endorsement contracts as they do from the tournaments they win. The sport has also become much more specialized. Serve-and-volley players tend to excel on hard courts and grass, while baseliners dominate clay-court competitions. In addition, the glamour and media attention connected to tennis have added a certain amount of pressure to the sport never seen before. Some have thrived under the spotlight, but others have burned out, quitting the sport from sheer exhaustion. Three players, however, have managed to continue playing through good and bad times. Each of them has taken the game in some way to a new level. And all of them are, in their own ways, true champions of the sport.

Boris Becker anxiously awaits the famously tough serve of Goran Ivanisevic at Wimbledon in 1991.

BORIS BECKER—
A PRODIGY COMES
OF AGE

The year: 1985. The scene: Centre Court at Wimbledon. The situation: one almost unheard of in the tournament's 112-year history. A player in the final match of the Gentleman's Singles competition was not only unseeded, but a mere boy. The lad's name was Boris Becker, and at 17 years of age he was about to become a tennis legend. At day's end, Becker had beaten Kevin Curren 6-3, 6-7, 7-6, 6-4 to become the tournament's youngest champion in history.

Was it a blessing or a curse? For Becker, the answer may have been both. From the moment he won the last point against Curren, expectations for Becker have been sky-high. At times he has thrived in the spotlight; at other times, it has made him anxious and angry.

Boris Becker was born in Leiman, Germany, in 1966. The son of a successful architect, he played for his high school tennis team. Becker was a prodigy from the start, and when he was 15, his high school coach called Ian Tiriac, a former pro from Romania, to take a look at the young red-headed player. Tiriac was impressed not only by Becker's talent, but by his desire. Becker ran down impossible shots and would not let a ball get past him without diving for it. By the end of a match his clothes would be filthy and his red hair full of dirt or clay, and sometimes blood dripped from a new wound on his knees or arms.

The following year, Becker dropped out of school to play tennis competitively. It took him only 12 months to play in his first Grand Slam event. And as you know by now, he came out of nowhere—an unseeded qualifier—to triumph. One of the reasons Becker played so effectively during this first competition was actually a technical one. In 1985, many players were still using old-fashioned rackets made of wood or steel. Becker was one of the first on the tour to use a midsize graphite racket. He was able to overpower many of his opponents simply by hitting the ball much harder than they were able to.

Boris showed his victory was no fluke when he repeated as Wimbledon champion the following year. The tournament in 1986 was a completely different—and much more difficult—experience for Becker from the 1985 competition. Suddenly he was the defending champion, and the eyes and ears of the media were watching. And under the glare of the attention, Becker emerged triumphant.

Becker's talent and competitive drive have kept him in the top ranks of the men's game for many years. On the other hand, Becker has had moments of frustration and embarrasing displays of emotion on court as well. At the 1987 Australian Open, for example, Becker disagreed often and vocally with the calls the line judge was making in his fourth-round match. After being warned several times and advised to limit his protests, Becker lost his temper completely, spitting water onto the court and throwing balls at the umpire. Becker was not ejected from the match (which he went on to lose), but he was fined for his behavior. In addition, much was made of his temper by the press. The media at this time had become accustomed to bursts of emotion and poor sportsmanship from Americans such as John McEnroe and Jimmy Connors, but a display from a European player was much less common.

Nevertheless, Becker has remained a contender and often a champion. Winless in Grand Slam events in 1987 and 1988, he won both the U.S. and Wimbledon crowns in 1989 and took top honors in Australia in 1991. And, rare for players of his generation, Becker has been a dependable and enthusiastic Davis Cup competitor for his country. He has played on the German team for 11 straight competitions, leading his country to victory in 1988.

Becker's style of play would have made Jack Kramer and his "big game" disciples proud. His overpowering serve allows him to rush to the net and put away points in what seems to be seconds. Becker's game is classic serve-and-volley, and when he's at the top of his game, passing Becker at the net is one of the most difficult challenges in the men's game.

ANDRE AGASSI:
IS IMAGE EVERYTHING?

In some ways, the story of Andre Agassi has been the exact opposite of that of Boris Becker. Famous before his first Grand Slam tournament, Agassi was always expected to win—long before he ever did.

That's not to say that Agassi did not have an impressive record in tournaments aside from Grand Slams. In fact, in 1988 he won enough championships on the professional tour to achieve the world's number-three ranking, even though his best Grand Slam finish that year was as a semifinalist at the French Open.

Andre Agassi was born in Las Vegas in 1970. His father, himself a former tennis player, introduced young Andre to the game at an early age—as soon as the youngest Agassi could hold a racket, he was swinging at a tennis ball his father had set up over his crib. His father was Andre's first tennis teacher, but by the time Andre was 16 he was the star player for Nick Bollettieri, a coach who ran a tennis academy for teenagers in Florida. It was there that Agassi perfected his game, which relied heavily on two-handed, pounding backhands and a brutal topspin forehand. Agassi rarely comes to the net, but he can make any opponent attempting to volley against him look foolish.

In 1986, Agassi reached the quarterfinals of a tournament in Stratton, Vermont, which had drawn media coverage because John McEnroe was making a comeback appearance at the same competition. Agassi won attention not only for his play on the court, but for his appearance and charisma as well. Unlike one's classic notion of a tennis player—dressed in all white, or at least in close-fitting cotton shorts and shirt—Agassi wore bright, flamboyant colors and baggy outfits. His hair was not only long but streaked several different colors. And he was an outgoing, laid-back personality who spoke easily to members of the press.

Andre Agassi first became famous for his outrageous style—wearing lots of jewelry, long hair, and brightly colored clothing on court. But he showed he had the heart of a champion when he won Wimbledon in 1992 and the U.S. Open in 1994.

After a forgettable year in 1987, Agassi went on a tear in 1988, when he broke through not only as a top-ten player but also as a new tennis celebrity. He was a popular spokesperson not only for tennis wear, but also for everyday products such as automobiles and cameras. His punch line for one of those commercials was one that would stick with Agassi for many years—"image is everything."

For Agassi, it did seem to be all image for the next few years. He would not grace the finals of a Grand Slam event once in the late 1980s (he reached the semifinals of the U.S. Open in 1988 and 1989). He did not play at Wimbledon during those years—claiming that it took away from his training time for the U.S. Open. He did play on the triumphant American Davis Cup team in 1988 and 1989, losing key singles matches in each competition. The following year he said that he would play on the American team again, then changed his mind and quit at the last minute.

By the end of 1991, many people were wondering about Agassi—he had gained weight, was seen at many late-night Hollywood parties, and on the whole had acted much more like a celebrity than an athlete. But the following year, Agassi quieted his critics in a very impressive fashion.

With a new coach, a new diet, training habits that whipped his body into shape, and—perhaps most important—a new attitude, Agassi made the decision to play in the 1992 Wimbledon championships. He was far from being the favorite to win; his backcourt game was much more fitting to slower surfaces than the grass of the Wimbledon courts. But Agassi played the best tennis of his career during the two-week tournament. When the dust had cleared, he was playing in his first Grand Slam final, against Goran Ivanisevic of Croatia, who was seeded higher than Agassi. At the end of the day, Agassi had used his pounding groundstrokes and quickness to win the match in four sets. Suddenly, it seemed, image was not everything. Agassi was for real—how else could he have won Wimbledon?

But Agassi did not win another Grand Slam title for two years, and he faded from prominence on the circuit by refusing to play in many of the tour's championships. By 1994, Agassi had slipped in the rankings to number 20 in the world. No one except his new girlfriend, actress Brooke Shields, thought he would do much at the U.S. Open. But Agassi's blistering returns and strategic play propelled him into the tournament's final, where he soared to his second Grand Slam tournament championship by beating Michael Stich in straight sets. And four months later, he became the number-one player in the world by winning the 1995 Australian Open.

The number-one ranking, however, was not his to keep. Agassi has struggled with his game in the late 1990s, and the top ranking was taken by another American—a young player named Pete Sampras.

PETE SAMPRAS—
BACK TO BASICS

Just when Americans were tiring of the loud and flamboyant behavior of such stars as Agassi, McEnroe, and Connors, along comes a quiet player who lets his racket do the talking and who can lose with as much grace (on the rare occasions it happens) as he displays when he wins. That player is Pete Sampras, who may be headed for the most impressive Grand Slam record of any male player in the open era.

Born in Potomac, Maryland, in 1970, Pete began playing with a racket at the age of three, hitting balls around the family's laundromat. In 1977, the family moved to Los Angeles, where his father enrolled seven-year-old Pete in the Jack Kramer tennis club. At 10, Pete played in his first tournament—and lost, 6-0, 6-0.

Discouraged but far from ready to retire, Pete kept playing and at 13 began practicing under the guidance of Dr. Pete Fischer, a pediatrician and tennis enthusiast. Fischer's favorite player was Rod Laver, and he aimed to teach Pete to play tennis in the Laver style—in both strategy and attitude. This meant switching Pete's backhand from a two-fisted backcourt style to a one-hander that would allow him to serve and volley more easily. The switch made Pete uncomfortable at first, but in the end it served its purpose.

By 1987, Sampras was playing junior tennis, and he gained his first major victory when he beat Michael Chang in the finals of the U.S. Open Junior championships. The next year, he joined the men's professional circuit and began his ascent up the men's ladder. Sampras's climb, however, had its share of pitfalls. In 1989, he reached the quarterfinals of the U.S. Open— upsetting defending champion Matts Wilander in the second round along the way—but then failed to get past the first round of the next three tournaments he played.

Even so, by the time the 1990 U.S. Open rolled

Pete Sampras is a master of the serve-and-volley game. Even if his opponent is able to return Sampras's blistering serve, Pete is usually right in position to win the point with a fiendish volley. Here Sampras shows his mastery at the 1994 Wimbledon competition, which he won.

around, Sampras had climbed to the number-12 ranking in the world. And at the age of 19, he was among the youngest on the top-20 list. Few had, in fact, heard of the well-behaved serve-and-volleyer who dressed all in white until he reached the semifinals, where he was slated to play John McEnroe. Many thought McEnroe was playing his best tennis in years. The U.S. Open

Sampras raises his arms in tri-umph after polishing off Andre Agassi at the 1995 U.S. Open. Experts predict that by the time Sampras retires, he will hold the record for most major victories.

that year was supposed to be a part of his come-back. Few thought Sampras had much of a chance. But Sampras outplayed his opponent, winning in straight sets. The next day he steam-rolled over Andre Agassi to take his first Grand Slam event and become a household name.

If the attention and media pressures have got-ten to Sampras over the years, he has rarely let it show on the court. Since winning the 1990 U.S. Open, Sampras has gone on to win nine more Grand Slam events. He has taken top hon-ors at the Australian Open in 1994 and 1997, and three consecutive championships at Wimbledon, in 1993, 1994, and 1995, plus another in 1997. Sampras's other three Grand Slam titles have come at the U.S. Open in 1993, 1995, and 1996.

In a way, it's not surprising that Sampras has never won the French Open. Like Boris Becker and John McEnroe, Sampras is a serve-and-volley player whose style is much more effective on the faster grass and hard court surfaces. The clay courts of France are much slower and more suited to a player who hits groundstrokes for long rallies, which is why backcourt specialists such as Thomas Muster and Sergi Bruguera play their best tennis there. Given the amount of specialization in the men's game today—there are serve-and-volley experts such as Sampras and Becker and groundstrokers like Agassi—it's no surprise that there have been no Grand Slam winners in tennis since Rod Laver in 1969.

Even so, many experts believe that if one player can do it, that man is Pete Sampras. His game can be overpowering at times, and when the time calls for it, he can beat opponents with finesse as well. His total of 10 Grand Slam tournament championships is second only to Bjorn Borg and Rod Laver in the Open era, each of whom won 11. And because Sampras is still fairly young, he may well be at the top of his game for several years to come.

FURTHER READING

Barlett, Michael, and Bob Gillen, eds. *The Tennis Book.* New York: Arbor House, 1981.

Bodo, Peter. *The Courts of Babylon.* New York: Scribner, 1995.

Evans, Richard. *Open Tennis 1968-1988: the Politics, the Pressures, the Passions, and the Great Matches.* Lexington, MA: The Stephen Green Press, 1988.

Feinstein, John. *Hard Courts.* New York: Random House, 1991.

Koster, Rich. *The Tennis Bubble.* New York: Quadrangle/The New York Times Book Co., Inc, 1976.

Trengrove, Alan. *The Story of the Davis Cup.* London: Stanley, Paul, and Co., 1985.

Winds, Herbert Warren. *Game, Set, and Match: The Tennis Book of the 1960s and 1970s.* New York: E.P. Dutton, 1979.

ABOUT THE AUTHOR

Paula Edelson is a freelance writer and journalist. She lives in Durham, North Carolina, with her husband and two sons. *Superstars of Men's Tennis* is her first book for Chelsea House.

INDEX